same
of different
As me.

same kind of different As me.

CONVERSATION GUIDE™

RON HALL *and* DENVER MOORE

THOMAS NELSON
Since 1798

Published in Nashville, Tennessee, by Thomas Nelson. Thomas Nelson is a
trademark of HarperCollins Christian Publishing, Inc.

The publisher would like to thank John Blase for his assistance in the writing
and development of this guide.

Thomas Nelson titles may be purchased in bulk for educational, business,
fund-raising, or sales promotional use. For information, please e-mail
SpecialMarkets@ThomasNelson.com.

ISBN: 9-781-4185-4287-0

First Printing January 2013 / Printed in the United States of America

contents

Introduction

What you have in your hands is a five-session guide designed as a complement to the *New York Times* best seller *Same Kind of Different as Me*. This guide is intended for use in a small group setting—one of mutual respect, confidentiality, and accountability.

Video segments are available for use with this resource, greatly enhancing the ongoing experience of this life-changing book.

You've probably heard the saying that there are two sides to every story. Well, in this case, there are three: Debbie Hall's, Ron Hall's, and Denver Moore's. As you move through this participant's guide, you'll hear these three voices and the jagged tale of their individual spiritual journeys, each one better for having followed Christ. But the goal is not to just observe; no, you'll be challenged to participate, to add your own voice to God's larger story, and to discover the difference you can make in someone's life—and the difference he or she can make in yours.

The five sessions are:

1. Extraordinary Faith

2. Forgiveness/Unconditional Love

3. Loving the Unlovable

4. Prayer

5. Blessing Versus Service

Each session will have a similar flow:

➤ **Introduction:** introductory words, followed by a pertinent quote

➤ **Getting Started:** a few lines of direction

➤ **Opening Chapters:** two or three excerpts from *Same Kind of Different as Me* (to be read aloud by a group member)

➤ **One-Liner:** a memorable saying from Denver, Ron, or Carson Hall

➤ **Exploration:** one or more biblical examples highlighting the session's theme (read by a group member)

➤ **Video:** a segment to be watched by the entire group

➤ **Reflection:** questions based on the content of the session and the video. There are two parts to this segment: (1) *Same as Me*—the discussion should revolve around the question, "How does what I just saw remind me of me?" and (2) *Different than Me*—here participants will ponder, "How does what I just saw differ from my experience?"

➤ **The Real World:** a concluding "real-world" challenge—that is, an opportunity to put the truth of each session into practice in the coming week while also being accountable to your group. This is the "homework" piece for each week.

So that everyone in your group will have ample time to engage with the questions, your leader has likely chosen to keep your group small. You may want to consult with your group leader before inviting additional guests to a session if your group leader has indicated yours will be a closed group. You should plan on meeting for at least ninety minutes for each session. Based on this material being structured for a group setting, it is wise to determine some ground rules. Your leader will guide you through this discussion during your first gathering.

- **Group Leader**—Each group should have a leader to coordinate the meeting times, to send reminders to everyone each week, to facilitate the times together, and to offer encouragement to the members of the group.

- **Confidentiality**—Determine the parameters that you as a group wish to observe. For example, each person's story is his or her own to tell, and it should be kept confidential. Accordingly, each person in the group should agree to not share another person's story with anyone else.

- **Open or Closed Group**—Determine whether you want a "closed" group or you will be open to bringing others into the group after it has begun. Because the original commitment is only for five sessions together, it is recommended that you maintain closed groups. Adding someone else in midstream when meeting for such a short time can be disruptive.

➤ **Confrontation**—Consider making a covenant allowing you freedom to speak into each other's lives. This will make it easier if things arise that need to be addressed. Implicit in this is that any confrontation will be done in a spirit of humility and gentleness.

extraordinary faith

There are those two four-letter words—HOPE and LOVE—and then there's that five-letter word—FAITH. While faith is not scripturally the greatest of these, it is quite possibly the hardest because its essence is the unseen, the not-yet, the still to come. And while trying to measure faith is an exercise in silliness, there do seem to be those moments in life when extraordinary faith is called for, something beyond the day-by-day trust we place in God.

"Faith is walking face-first and full-speed into the dark."

—**Elizabeth Gilbert**

GETTING STARTED

Following are two excerpts highlighting extraordinary faith, from the book *Same Kind of Different as Me*. As a group, take turns reading each excerpt aloud, paying attention to any key words or phrases that catch your attention. When you are finished reading, take a few minutes to share your thoughts with the group.

OPENING CHAPTERS

The first excerpt concerns a dream Debbie Hall had that is really the core of the story of *Same Kind of Different as Me*.

> She did have one other fear, though: missing the call of God. And she felt called to work at the mission. I wish I could say I felt God had tapped me for the

assignment, too, but I didn't. But I did feel called to be a good husband, so I went.

The Union Gospel Mission sits just beyond the beauty of the restored section of Fort Worth, a city that became a national model for downtown revitalization, thanks to the billionaires who loved it. In that part of town, soaring glass towers pulse with legal intrigue and high finance. Nearby, warmer-looking buildings refaced with brick and brownstone line sidewalks graced with raised iron flowerboxes, manicured trees, and—after all, it's Texas—topiaries of longhorn cattle. A cultural district spans three city blocks, housing three world-class museums, the Kimbell, the Amon Carter, and the Modern. A mile east, cafés open onto cobblestone plazas where dazzling urbanites can sip lattes and mineral water, and watch cowboys amble by in their boots and spurs.

Travel farther east, though, and the colors and flora of restoration fade into hopelessness and despair. Drive under the I-30/I-35 interchange, pass beneath an impossible pretzel of freeways called the Mixmaster and through a tunnel that efficiently separates the haves from the unsightly have-nots, and there are no more plazas or monuments or flowerboxes and certainly no more dazzling urbanites. In their place:

tumbledown buildings with busted-out glass. Walls scarred with urine stains and graffiti. Gutters choked with beer cans and yellowed newspapers. And vacant lots blanketed in johnsongrass tall enough to conceal a sea of empty vodka bottles and assorted drunks.

Driving out of that tunnel shocks most people into realizing they made a wrong turn. But on a sun-splashed Monday in the early spring of 1998, Deborah and I drove out there on purpose, she propelled by her passion to help the broken and I propelled by a love for my wife.

As we passed out of the dark tunnel onto East Lancaster Street, we witnessed a curious one-way migration, a streaming of people, like tributaries all flowing east into a single, larger river of souls. On our left, a string of shabby men staggered from the johnsongrass that covered a lot. To the right, a parade of women and children in dirty, mismatched clothes shambled along, dragging green garbage bags. One boy, about eight, wore only a man's undershirt and black socks.

"They're going to the mission!" Deborah said, beaming, as if the entire ragtag bunch was long-lost TCU alumni and she just couldn't wait to catch up. I managed some sort of agreeing noise and a thin smile.

To me, they looked as if they'd somehow found a portal from the Middle Ages and squeaked through just in time to escape the plague.

When we reached the mission, I bumped our truck over the driveway dip where a brown-trousered fat man dangled a cigarette from his lips and stood guard at a rusted chain-link gate. I offered my friendliest east Texas grin. "We're here to volunteer," I told him.

He flashed back a toothless smile, and I swear his cigarette never moved, just clung to his bottom lip as though he'd tacked it there with a stapler.

I had pulled into the parking lot wondering how quickly I'd be able to pull out again, but Deborah suddenly spoke in a tone that you learn to recognize when you've loved someone for years, a tone that says, "Hear me on this."

"Ron, before we go in, I want to tell you something." She leaned back against her headrest, closed her eyes. "I picture this place differently than it is now. White flowerboxes lining the streets, trees and yellow flowers. Lots of yellow flowers like the pastures at Rocky Top in June."

Deborah opened her eyes and turned to me with an expectant smile: "Can't you just *see* that?

No vagrants, no trash in the gutters, just a beautiful place where these people can know God loves them as much as He loves the people on the other side of that tunnel."

I smiled, kissed my fingertips, and laid them against her cheek. "Yes, I can see that." And I could. I just didn't mention that I thought she was getting a little ahead of herself.

She hesitated, then spoke again. "I had a dream about it."

"About this place?"

"Yes," she said, gazing at me intently. "I saw this place changed. It was beautiful, like I was saying, with the flowers and everything. It was crystal clear, like I was standing right here and it was the future already."

*   *   *

The second excerpt describes an incredibly painful time in the history of Denver Moore, an experience that could have embittered him forever had it not been for the mustard seed of faith in his life and the lives of those around him.

I was just puttin the lug nuts back on when them three boys rode outta the woods and asked the lady did she need any help. 'Course, the redheaded fella with the big teeth was the one that first spotted me and called me a nigger. And the next thing I knew, I had a rope squeezed tight around my neck and black terror slitherin through my belly like a water moccasin.

"We gon' teach you a lesson about botherin white ladies," said the one holdin the rope.

'Cept I hadn't been botherin her, just fixin her tire. But she didn't volunteer no other story, and I didn't say nothin 'cause for sure they wadn't gon' be believin me. I figured if I spoke, it would just add to my troubles.

I kept an eye on the boy with the rope, and when he lashed it to his saddle, I knowed what was comin and got real scared. With both hands, I reached up to try to get the rope loose. That's when they snapped their reins and took off just a-laughin.

The horses trotted at first, goin slow enough for me to run. I was stumblin along behind, my hands still graspin at the noose and me tryin to keep my feet under me. The horses was only maybe ten feet in front of me, and I could hear their feet beatin the dirt. The dust stung my eyes. I could taste it.

Then I heard a whoop and a holler. My feet flew out from under me and I crashed down in the dirt, my knees and elbows skiddin down the road. The horses pounded and pounded and I held on to the noose like a steerin wheel, tryin to pry my fingers inside of it to keep the noose from closin in tighter. The dirt was blindin me and chokin me. My shirtsleeves and the knees of my britches tore away, then my skin peeled back like a rabbit ready for the skillet. I couldn't hear no more laughin, just the terrible thunder of them horses draggin me down to die.

I expect I would a' died if Bobby and his aunt, the Man's wife from the other plantation, hadn't been drivin down the road right then. I'd about blacked out by that time, and I don't really remember too much of what happened next. I just know the draggin all of a sudden stopped. I peeked through my eyes, which had swoll up to slits and seen Bobby's aunt standin in the road pointin a shotgun at them boys on horses.

"Cut him loose!" she hollered. I felt the noose go slack and seen the raggedy end of the rope fall to the ground like a snake with the evil gone out of it. Then I heard them boys ride off laughin.

Bobby and his aunt hustled me into their car and drove me to my auntie's house. She tended to me with her roots and potions, slatherin a paste on my eyes to ease the swellin. I stayed in her bed a week till the swellin went down and I could see good again. Took about that long for my skin to scab over so I could put on pants and a shirt.

I knowed who done it. And I figured their daddies was in the Klan. But in Red River Parish, colored men had learned it was better to keep their mouths shut than tell what they know, 'less they wanted worse things to happen to their family, like maybe wakin up in the middle of the night with the house on fire.

Lookin back, I figure what them boys done caused me to get a little throwed off in life. And for sure I wadn't gon' be offerin to help no white ladies no more.

ONE-LINER

Read the following statement and the section below, and then discuss as a group.

"Mommy, I ran out of strong."

—**Carson Hall**

Debbie and Ron's son, Carson, used this phrase as a little boy; it described times when he felt extra tired. Can you relate to being *out of strong*? It could be a physical tiredness or an emotional or spiritual weariness, or it could be some combination of all of the above. In other words, you've exhausted all the possibilities, and you've come to the end of your rope, maybe even the end of yourself. As Denver would say, "Our limitation is God's opportunity."

Extraordinary faith is stepping out into a situation or experience to which God is calling you when you don't have the strength or smarts to go on, when you've *run out of strong*. That's the point at which God can take over and work and move in ways that can only be ascribed to Him and His glory.

EXPLORATION

Matthew 8 contains two stories of contrasting faith: one tells of a centurion, a man under authority who displayed a confidence in Jesus and His power to heal, while the other tells of an incident in the lives of the disciples. As a group member reads aloud, pay close attention to these stories in light of the earlier excerpts.

The Faith of the Centurion

> Now when Jesus had entered Capernaum, a centurion came to Him, pleading with Him, saying, "Lord, my servant is lying at home paralyzed, dreadfully tormented."
>
> And Jesus said to him, "I will come and heal him."
>
> The centurion answered and said, "Lord, I am not worthy that You should come under my roof. But only speak a word, and my servant will be healed. For I also am a man under authority, having soldiers under me. And I say to this one, 'Go,' and he goes; and to another, 'Come,' and he comes; and to my servant, 'Do this,' and he does it."
>
> When Jesus heard it, He marveled, and said to those who followed, "Assuredly, I say to you, I have not found such great faith, not even in Israel!" (Matthew 8:5–10)

* * *

Jesus Calms the Storm

Now when He got into a boat, His disciples followed Him. And suddenly a great tempest arose on the sea, so that the boat was covered with the waves. But He was asleep. Then His disciples came to Him and awoke Him, saying, "Lord, save us! We are perishing!"

But He said to them, "Why are you fearful, O you of little faith?" Then He arose and rebuked the winds and the sea, and there was a great calm.

So the men marveled, saying, "Who can this be, that even the winds and the sea obey Him?" (Matthew 8:23–27)

After seeing the centurion's level of trust, Jesus qualified his faith as *great*, or you could say *extraordinary*. But the word used to describe His own disciples' faith was *little*. Not really what you might expect, is it?

Extraordinary faith. *Great* faith. And for a little different variation on that theme, Ron mentioned that Debbie had a *scary* faith, one that not only challenged him but unsettled him as well. Take a moment and consider that last adjective—*scary*. First off, what do you find *scary*?

Don't overthink it; just go with what comes immediately to mind, and share with the group. Then, what are some ways that FAITH can be scary, not only to yourself but also to those around you? Give yourself a moment to think before sharing.

VIDEO

If you'd like to take a few notes as you watch the session 1 video segment, use the space below.

REFLECTION

During this section it is time to open up and discover how God might use this session to transform your life.

Same as Me

> ➤ When you consider the time you placed your faith in Christ, did it look more like Debbie's (well researched/C. S. Lewis-like) or Ron's (rather quick and immediate/Damascus road-like)? Share a little bit about that experience.

➤ What are some of the dreams you have for your life? They may be personal or corporate or both. Do you feel that any of those dreams are God-ordained, something you *have* to do, and that they might call for *extraordinary faith?*

Different than Me

➤ Ron and Debbie Hall were Texans, accustomed to a certain lifestyle, living in the bustling metropolis of Dallas/Fort Worth. That's their story. What is

yours? Where do you find yourself in life at this time?
Be as specific as you can.

➤ Initially, Denver was skittish around Ron and Debbie,
not really knowing their intentions. What about you?
Has there been a time when someone significant to
your life reached out to help or befriend you, but you
initially kept that person at arm's length? Share briefly
about that time. How can that memory inform some
of your own attempts at helping in the present?

THE REAL WORLD

As you close this session, take a few moments and come up with two ways you can practice *extraordinary* or even *scary* FAITH this week. As you think about those scenarios, who are the other characters involved—family, friends, coworkers? If you had to guess, what would some of their reactions be to your exercise of risky faith? Will they be supportive? Surprised? Might they just walk away? As you share your thoughts, remember that you are committing to the other members of the group an intention to actually try to exercise a level of faith that's uncommon for you.

Here are two words of encouragement: start small; don't try to change the other person or the world or yourself overnight. And remember Philippians 4:13, but at the same time, don't forget that verse 14 reminds us that when we *run out of strong,* God wants to strengthen us by the presence and support of our brothers and sisters in the body of Christ. After everyone has had a chance to share, take a few minutes to pray, asking God to bless the group's efforts at extraordinary faith in the week ahead.

"I can do all things through Christ who strengthens me. Nevertheless you have done well that you shared in my distress."

—Philippians 4:13-14

forgiveness / unconditional love

INTRODUCTION

Most of us have *the one*, that thing about which we think, *If I ever did* that, *I could never be forgiven, much less forgive myself.* Whatever else the one thing may be, it is a boundary, a limit, a condition stating, *Don't go beyond this point.* But in the heat of some moments, we often disregard that voice in our heads that says, *Don't do it!*—and we do it. And that's when life gets really interesting, isn't it?

"One of the keys to happiness is a bad memory."
—**Rita Mae Brown**

GETTING STARTED

Following are two excerpts highlighting forgiveness/
unconditional love, from the book *Same Kind of Different as Me*. As a group, take turns reading each excerpt aloud, paying attention to any key words or phrases that catch your attention. When you are finished reading, take a few minutes to share your thoughts with the group.

OPENING CHAPTERS

In both of the opening chapters that follow, Ron Hall is the recipient of forgiveness. In the first scenario, Ron knew exactly why forgiveness was needed; his wrong was clear. But the second scenario is not quite as clear, and Ron needed Denver to help him "wake up."

In the end, I saw the artist only twice, once in California and once in New York, then confessed to

Deborah—with a little help from my friends. I confided my conquest to a friend, who confided my confidence to his wife, who "encouraged" me to tell Deborah. If I didn't, she said, she would.

Calculating that it was better to rat myself out than look like a weasel, I called the artist from the office one day and told her I couldn't see her anymore. Then I went home and confessed to Deborah. My spin: Her disinterest had driven me into the arms of another woman, one who wanted me just the way I was—money and all.

"What!" she screamed, flying into a rage. "Nineteen years! Nineteen years! What were you thinking? How could you do this?"

Shoes, vases, and figurines flew through the air, some a direct hit. When nothing else presented itself as a weapon, Deborah pounded me with her bare fists until her arms wore out and hung limp at her sides.

The night spun by in a whirl of sleepless anger. The next morning we phoned our pastor, then drove to his office where we spent most of the day airing our garbage. In the end, we discovered that neither of us was quite ready to give up. We did still love each other, though in that vestigial way of couples who've worn each other out. We agreed to try to work things out.

Back at the house that night, we were sitting in our bedroom retreat, talking, when Deborah asked me something that nearly made me faint. "I want to talk to her. Will you give me her phone number?"

Deborah's resolve at that moment was like a student skydiver who, once at altitude, strides straight to the plane's open door and leaps without pausing to bat down the butterflies. She picked up the bedroom phone and punched each number as I recited it.

"This is Deborah Hall, Ron's wife," she said calmly into the phone.

I tried to imagine the shocked face on the other end of the line.

"I want you to know that I don't blame you for the affair with my husband," Deborah went on. "I know that I've not been the kind of wife Ron needed, and I take responsibility for that."

She paused, listening.

Then: "I want you to know that I forgive you," Deborah said. "I hope you find someone who will not only truly love you but honor you."

Her grace stunned me. But not nearly so much as what she said next: "I intend to work on being the best wife Ron could ever want, and if I do my job right, you will not be hearing from my husband again."

Deborah quietly placed the phone in its cradle, sighed with relief, and locked her eyes on mine. "You and I are now going to rewrite the future history of our marriage."

She wanted to spend a couple of months in counseling, she said, so we could figure out what was broken, how it got that way, and how to fix it. "If you'll do that," she said, "I'll forgive you. And I promise I will never bring this up, ever again."

It was a gracious offer, considering that I, and not Deborah, had been the traitor. Faster than you can say "divorce court," I said yes. . . .

*　*　*

Denver was first to break the silence. "What's your name again?"

"Ron."

"And what's your wife's name?"

"Deborah."

"Mr. Ron and Miss Debbie," he said, allowing a smile to escape. "I'll try to remember."

Then his smile faded into seriousness, as if he'd had a rare light moment then someone had closed the blinds. He stared down at the steam rolling up from his coffee cup. "I been thinkin a lot about what you asked me."

I had no idea what he was talking about. "What did I ask you?"

"'Bout bein your friend."

My jaw dropped an inch. I'd forgotten that when I told him at the Cactus Flower Café that all I wanted from him was his friendship, he'd said he'd think about it. Now, I was shocked that anyone would spend a week pondering such a question. While the whole conversation had slipped my mind, Denver had clearly spent serious time preparing his answer.

He looked up from his coffee, fixing me with one eye, the other squinted like Clint Eastwood. "There's somethin I heard 'bout white folks that bothers me, and it has to do with fishin."

He was serious and I didn't dare laugh, but I did try to lighten the mood a bit. "I don't know if I'll be able to help you," I said, smiling. "I don't even own a tackle box."

Denver scowled, not amused. "I think you can."

He spoke slowly and deliberately, keeping me pinned with that eyeball, ignoring the Starbucks groupies coming and going on the patio around us. "I heard that when white folks go fishin they do some-thin called 'catch and release.'"

Catch and release? I nodded solemnly, suddenly nervous and curious at the same time.

"That really bothers me," Denver went on. "I just can't figure it out. 'Cause when colored folks go fishin, we really proud of what we catch, and we take it and show it off to everybody that'll look. Then we eat what we catch . . . in other words, we use it to *sustain* us. So it really bothers me that white folks would go to all that trouble to catch a fish, then when they done caught it, just throw it back in the water."

He paused again, and the silence between us stretched a full minute. Then: "Did you hear what I said?"

I nodded, afraid to speak, afraid to offend.

Denver looked away, searching the blue autumn sky, then locked onto me again with that drill-bit stare. "So, Mr. Ron, it occurred to me: If you is fishin for a friend you just gon' catch and release, then I ain't got no desire to be your friend."

The world seemed to halt in midstride and fall silent around us like one of those freeze-frame scenes on TV. I could hear my heart pounding and imagined Denver could see it popping my breast pocket up and down. I returned Denver's gaze with what I hoped was a receptive expression and hung on.

Suddenly his eyes gentled and he spoke more softly than before: "But if you is lookin for a *real* friend, then I'll be one. Forever."

ONE-LINER

Read the following statement and the section below, and then discuss as a group.

"We all need forgiveness."

—Denver Moore

In Ron and Debbie's story, infidelity was the straw that could have broken the camel's back. But it didn't. Debbie's forgiveness and unconditional love toward Ron can only be described as Christlike: swift and complete—as far as the east is from the west. Such grace is stunning indeed, and unfortunately quite rare. There was also a beautiful picture of forgiveness when Ron saw the fallacy of the usual catch-and-release approach to people, an approach in which Denver had no interest. While we often talk of God's "forgiveness" with ease, that word really begins to mean something when another human being extends it to us, when someone we've offended or hurt becomes God-with-skin-on. What do you think of Denver's line "We all need forgiveness"?

EXPLORATION

There's probably no forgiveness story more poignant than that found in John 8—the story of the woman caught in the act of adultery. Most translations indicate this story as a later addition to the text, but it tracks hand in glove with the character of Jesus; it is in no way inauthentic.

A Woman Caught in Adultery

Then the scribes and Pharisees brought to Him a woman caught in adultery. And when they had set her in the midst, they said to Him, "Teacher, this woman was caught in adultery, in the very act. Now Moses, in the law, commanded us that such should be stoned. But what do You say?" This they said, testing Him, that they might have something of which to accuse Him. But Jesus stooped down and wrote on the ground with His finger, as though He did not hear.

So when they continued asking Him, He raised Himself up and said to them, "He who is without sin among you, let him throw a stone at her first." And again He stooped down and wrote on the ground. Then those who heard it, being convicted by their conscience, went out one by one, beginning with the oldest even to the last. And Jesus was left alone, and the woman standing in the midst. When Jesus had raised Himself up and saw no one but the woman, He said to her, "Woman, where are those accusers of yours? Has no one condemned you?"

She said, "No one, Lord."

And Jesus said to her, "Neither do I condemn you; go and sin no more." (verses 3–11)

Do you recall Debbie's words to Ron in the excerpt earlier? "I'll forgive you. And I promise I will never bring this up, ever again." It sounds an awful lot like the way Jesus forgave the adulterous woman: swiftly and completely. While you might sense the challenge here as forgiving someone who has wronged you in some way, the challenge could equally be receiving forgiveness from somebody you've done wrong. At the end of the day, as Denver says, *We all need forgiveness.* If a few group members are willing to share similar stories, take a few moments to hear about that person who was God-with-skin-on to them.

VIDEO

If you'd like to take a few notes as you watch the session 2 video segment, use the space below.

REFLECTION

During this section it is time to open up and discover how God might use this session to transform your life.

Same as Me

- In light of this session's focus on forgiveness, who do you relate to more in your current season of life— Debbie or Ron? In other words, are you the forgiver or the one needing forgiveness?

- Would you say that's been the case in the past, or has that changed somewhat? If so, how or why did it change? Share as much as you're comfortable sharing, no more.

Different than Me

➤ Which is harder for you, giving or receiving forgiveness? Has that always been the case, or did something shift along the way? Do you believe that's true for most people? Why or why not?

➤ Music is a universal language. Choose a song lyric that you feel best represents forgiveness and unconditional love. Take a few moments and share with the group.

THE REAL WORLD

If you've got a pulse, chances are good you've offended or been offended by someone in the last several weeks. Share the offense and what you've done or not done about it. Ask the group for their input into the situation, and commit to taking at least a step in the direction of forgiveness. If you've already taken a first step, what would be the next one?

A final thought: Take care not to place a value on an offense; for example, if adultery is a 10, then a friend disagreeing with you about some recent event is a 4. That kind of grading system is rarely helpful for anyone. "Suck it up, buttercup" may work well in the movies, but this is the real world. Diminishing another's experience is not the stuff of which successful small groups are made. Remember, it's about loving without condition. After everyone's had an opportunity to share, conclude this week's session with silent prayer. The group leader can say amen after a minute or so.

"Bearing with one another, and forgiving one another, if anyone has a complaint against another; even as Christ forgave you, so you also must do."

—Colossians 3:13

loving the unlovable

Prejudice. Merriam-Webster defines the word as "an adverse opinion or leaning formed without just grounds or before sufficient knowledge." Most of us would like to believe we're not prejudiced, but we betray ourselves in numerous ways each day. We prejudge places and things and worst of all, people. The only way to gain ground that's "just" or knowledge that is "sufficient" is to step outside of your life and into another's.

Although the phrase is well-worn, it's about the best descriptor there is: "stepping outside your comfort zone."

So loving the unlovable is going to be uncomfortable, at least at first and possibly for quite a while. But such is the nature of love.

"To love means loving the unlovable."

—G. K. Chesterton

GETTING STARTED

Following are two excerpts highlighting loving the unlovable, from the book *Same Kind of Different as Me*. This week, try reading the excerpts by paragraphs, allowing each member an opportunity to read. Pay attention to any key words or phrases that catch your attention. When you are finished reading, take a few minutes to share your thoughts with the group.

OPENING CHAPTERS

The chapters that follow were uncomfortable for Ron, and chances are good they may even be somewhat uncomfortable to read. But such is the nature of love.

At first the daisy chain of wilted souls who shuffled by for their Tuesday handouts depressed me. The first in line were mamas with their children, most of whom wore stained, ill-fitting clothes and looked like someone had cut their hair with a kitchen knife. Next came a string of women ages eighteen to eighty-five, followed by the "old" men, many younger than I, but with creased and haggard faces that made them look ancient. After that, the younger men, some beaten and sullen, some hiding behind a loud, false cheer meant to mask their shame. These were the ones who wandered the streets all day, then slept at the mission.

Last to eat were the undiluted street people, shabby and pungent. It took me a while to get over their smell, which floated in their wake like the noxious cloud around a chemical plant. The odor seemed to stick to the hairs inside my nose. I swore I could see the hair on some of their heads rustling, jostled by hidden armies of squirming lice. A couple of the men had stumps protruding where an arm or a leg used to be. One long-haired fellow wore a necklace fashioned from several hundred cigarette butts tied together with string. He wore black plastic garbage bags tied to his belt loops. I didn't want to know what was in them.

On our first day, Deborah, surveying the street people, looked at me and said, "Let's call them 'God's people.'"

I was thinking they looked more like the extras in the movie *Mad Max Beyond Thunderdome*.

Everyone who ate at the mission earned their free meal only after going into the chapel to sit like dead men on hard benches while a white-haired and nearly blind preacher named Brother Bill roared about the saving power of Jesus and the unpleasant consequences reserved for the unredeemed. From the kitchen side of the chapel door—locked to prevent altar-call escapees—I could hear the hellfire-and-brimstone, tough-love message that I agree often cracks hard cases. But it seemed manipulative to me to make the hungry sit like good dogs for their supper. And it did not surprise me that even when Brother Bill split the air with one of his more rousing sermons, not a single soul ever burst through the chapel doors waving their hands and praising Jesus. At least not while we were there.

The men and women we served seemed pleasantly surprised to have a smiling couple with all their teeth serving them supper. I'm sure they thought Deborah was on amphetamines, or possibly running for mayor, as they had likely never seen anyone who smiled and asked after them as much as she did. . . .

*   *   *

When we entered Mr. Ballantine's room at the nursing home, the smell hit me first—the stench of age, dead skin, and bodily fluids. The old man lay on his bed in a puddle of urine, naked except for a neon orange ski jacket. His ghostly chicken-bone legs sprawled across a sheet that had once been white but now was dingy gray, streaked with brown and ocher stains. Around him lay strewn trash and trays of half-eaten food . . . scrambled eggs, crusted hard-yellow . . . shriveled meats . . . petrified sandwiches. On a couple of trays, school-lunch-size milk cartons, tipped over, the puddles congealed into stinking clabber.

In a single, sweeping glance, Denver sized up the room, then me, wobbling and on the verge of vomit. "Mr. Ron just come to say hi," he told Mr. Ballantine. "He got to be goin now."

I bolted, leaving Denver alone to clean up Mr. Ballantine and his nasty room. I didn't offer to help, or even to stay and pray. Feeling guilty, but not guilty enough to change, I jumped in my car and wept as I drove away—for Mr. Ballantine, homeless and decrepit, who would stew in his own excrement if not for Denver; and I wept for myself, because I didn't have the courage to stay. It was easy for someone like me to serve a few meals, write a few checks, and get my name and picture in the paper for showing up at some glitzy benefit. But Denver served invisibly, loved without fanfare. The tables had turned, and I now feared that it was he who would catch-and-release me, a person who lacked true compassion, who perhaps wasn't a catch worth keeping.

I gained a new and more profound respect for Denver that day, my perception of him changing like puzzle pieces slowly clicking into place. He wasn't showing off, only sharing with me a secret part of his life. Had his secrets included pitching dice in an alley with a hoard of drunken bums, I wouldn't have been put off. But I was shocked that they included not only praying through the night for my wife, but also nursing this man who never said thank you and continued to call him "nigger."

For the first time, it struck me that when Denver said he'd be my friend for life, he meant it—for better or for worse. The hell of it was, Mr. Ballantine never wanted a friend, especially a black one. But once Denver committed, he stuck. It reminded me of what Jesus told His disciples: "Greater love has no man than this, that he lay down his life for his friends."

ONE-LINER

Read the following statement and move directly into the **Exploration** section; then discuss as a group.

"You never know whose eyes God is watching you through."

—**Denver Moore**

EXPLORATION

Listen closely as a group member reads this passage aloud. For some it will be a very familiar passage; all the more reason to pay close attention.

The Good Samaritan

"And who is my neighbor?"

Then Jesus answered and said: "A certain man went down from Jerusalem to Jericho, and fell among thieves, who stripped him of his clothing, wounded him, and departed, leaving him half dead. Now by chance a certain priest came down that road. And when he saw him, he passed by on the other side. Likewise a Levite, when he arrived at the place, came and looked, and passed by on the other side. But a certain Samaritan, as he journeyed, came where he was. And when he saw him, he had compassion. So he went to him and bandaged his wounds, pouring on oil and wine; and he set him on his own animal, brought him to an inn, and took care of him. On the next day, when he departed, he took out two denarii, gave them to the innkeeper, and said to him, 'Take care of him;

and whatever more you spend, when I come again, I will repay you.' So which of these three do you think was neighbor to him who fell among the thieves?"

And he said, "He who showed mercy on him."

Then Jesus said to him, "Go and do likewise." (Luke 10:29–37)

Before stepping into Denver's life, Ron had always looked at the homeless with a question similar to that of the priest and the Levite: "What might possibly happen to me if I stopped to help?" Debbie, on the other hand, always asked a very good Samaritan-style question: "What might happen to them if I don't stop to help?" One approach, Ron's, was based on self-preservation. The other, Debbie's, was based on self-sacrifice. Jesus agrees with Debbie's approach and says, "Go and do likewise." Which character are you, most of the time—the priest? Levite? Samaritan?

VIDEO

If you'd like to take a few notes as you watch the session 3 video segment, use the space below.

REFLECTION

During this section it is time to open up and discover how God might use this session to transform your life.

Same as Me

➤ Think for a moment about your city or town or maybe even your neighborhood. What people are considered "trash"? Sure, they're not called that in public, but it's obvious that kind of prejudice exists; so who is "trash"?

➤ Ron stated that "God took what our city deemed trash and turned it into a national treasure." But God used Ron and Debbie and others to accomplish that transformation. Do you feel God needs or wants you to be involved in a similar story? Why or why not?

Different than Me

➤ Recall an instance when you acted like the priest and the Levite: you "passed by on the other side." Was it a long time ago or in the recent past? What kinds of feelings arise when remembering that time?

➤ Recall a time when you were the one, figuratively or literally, beaten and robbed and left half-dead. Was there a good woman or man who came along and bandaged you up? If so, honor that person by naming him or her and expressing gratitude for the courageous love that "good Samaritan" showed. If not, grieve that experience by sharing it with your group members.

THE REAL WORLD

Ron described Denver as being "in the recycling business." As Christians, we all are. Name one person in your life who needs recycling. Now, we all do to some extent, but this person is the one who comes to mind often, who just sorta gnaws at your conscience, that person who seems to be watching you for some reason. Share a little about the situation, and listen for any group input that might help you as you take what will be uncomfortable steps.

Be aware that, yes, God may be inviting you into the life of a homeless person. But also be aware that God may be asking you to get involved in the recycling of a family member or friend who may not necessarily be homeless but is definitely in the category of those who consider themselves unlovable. But that person is one of God's people, one of His friends.

"Greater love has no one than this, than to lay down one's life for his friends."

—John 15:13

prayer

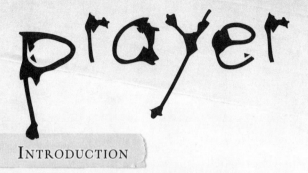

When the disciples said, "Lord, teach us to pray" (Luke 11:1), He responded by giving them a succinct guide to the Christian life. And while each line is vital, the prayer begins with a surrender—"Your will be done" (verse 2). Our tendency is to place "my will be done" in parentheses, just off to the side, thinking that surely God's will and our will are synonymous.

"May all your expectations be frustrated, may all your plans be thwarted, may all your desires be withered into nothingness, that you may experience the powerlessness and poverty

of a child and sing and dance in the love of
God who is the Father, Son and Spirit."

—Brennan Manning, quoting Larry Hein

GETTING STARTED

This week's excerpts focus on prayer. As Debbie Hall walked not only *through* but *into* the valley of the shadow of death, the two men in her life—Ron and Denver—went through an intensive session in the classroom of prayer. They discovered that the line does indeed read, "*Your* will be done."

OPENING CHAPTERS

As a group member reads these excerpts, try to assume a posture of prayer, not necessarily on bended knee but maybe with eyes closed and head bowed.

"This is Deborah's liver," Dr. Burk explained, drawing an invisible circle around a shape on the screen.

Then I saw them: shadows. Her liver was completely covered with them.

As we stared at the film, several more doctors filtered into the room, their white coats and serious faces vaguely blue in the dim light. A couple of them experimented with sounding upbeat.

"These spots are a little troubling, but it's nothing to worry about yet," said one.

"It's possible they're birthmarks," said another. "I've seen that before."

But none of them looked us in the eye. The word *cancer* floated through my mind like a poisonous gas, but I didn't dare utter it.

"We've scheduled a colonoscopy for tomorrow morning," Craig said. They would withhold judgment until then.

At home that night, we settled into bed, and Deborah shared with me the story of Joshua and Caleb, two of twelve men Moses sent to spy out the Promised Land and bring back a report for the children of Israel.

We lay facing each other, heads on white-cased pillows. "When the spies came back, they brought good news and bad news," Deborah said, her voice lilting softly like a storyteller. "The good news was that the land *did* flow with milk and honey, just as God had promised. The bad news was that the land was inhabited by giants." The Israelites wept with fear, she went on, all except for Joshua and Caleb, who said, "If the Lord is pleased with us, He will give us the land. Do not be afraid."

Deborah fell silent for a few minutes, then raised her eyes to mine. "Ron, I'm afraid."

I pulled her to me and held her. We prayed about the colonoscopy. That the Lord would be pleased with us, that the doctors would bring back a good report.

* * *

Stars hung like ice in a black sky when we pulled into the All Saints parking lot the next morning. Word of Deborah's pending diagnosis had spread among our friends, and we were surprised and touched to find about twenty of them clustered in the day surgery waiting room, praying.

As the doctors wheeled Deborah away and she made her pale face brave, we prayed for a good report. I posted myself outside the door of the endoscopy room—as close to Deborah as they'd let me get—and paced the cold tile floors. I alternated between prayer and mild panic, between "the peace of God that surpasses all understanding" and bubbling nausea. An eon ticked by, then an epoch. Sand through an hourglass a grain at a time.

Finally, through the square of wired safety glass, I saw nurses wheeling Deborah into recovery and rushed to join her. Through heavily lidded eyes, she looked up at me, her bottom lip protruding slightly in a way it did only when she was truly sad. She mouthed the word *cancer*, her lips attempting a half-smile to cushion the blow.

Then tiny tears appeared in the corners of her eyes and spilled down her pale cheeks and I remembered her words from the night before: *giants in the Promised Land. . . .*

* * *

I guess I coulda prayed in my bed, but I felt like I was keepin watch, and I didn't want to fall asleep like Jesus's disciples in the garden. And I coulda prayed in the chapel, but I didn't want nobody comin round breakin my concentration. I knowed wadn't nobody gon' come around the Dumpster, so that's where I kept watch over Miss Debbie ever night, what they call a "vigil."

I sat on the ground with my back propped up against the brick wall of an old building where the Dumpster was at and looked up into the dark sky and talked to God about her. I asked Him a lot to heal her, and I also asked Him why. Why have You afflicted this woman who has been nothin but a faithful servant to You? Someone who is doin what You said, visitin the sick, feedin the hungry, invitin the stranger in? How come You bring this heartache to her family and cut off the love she be givin to the homeless?

It didn't make no sense to me. But after a while, God explained it. A lotta times while I was out there, I'd see a shootin star burn across the black sky, bright one minute and gone the next. Ever time I seen one, seemed like it was gon' fall all the way to the ground, and I couldn't understand why I never could see where it went. After I seen a lot of em act that way, I felt like God was givin me a message 'bout Miss Debbie.

The Word says God put ever star in the heavens and even give ever one of em a name. If one of em was gon' fall out the sky, that was up to Him, too. Maybe we can't see where it's gon' wind up, but He can.

That's when I knew that even though it didn't make no sense to me, God had put Miss Debbie in my life like a bright star, and God knew where she was gon' wind up. And I found out that sometimes we just have to accept the things we don't understand. So I just tried to accept that Miss Debbie was sick and kept on prayin out there by that Dumpster. I felt like it was the most important job I ever had, and I wadn't gon' quit.

ONE-LINER

Read the following statement and the section below; then discuss as a group.

"Nothin ever really ends but something new don't begin."
—Denver Moore

In the passage that follows, Mary and Martha's "my will" was obvious: that Jesus come and save their brother, Lazarus. But pray as they did, that didn't happen, at least not according to their plan. And these two sisters, women dear to the heart of Christ, fell into the ditch of "if"—"If You had been here . . ." What are some "if-ditches" in your life right now? Remember, there are no silly answers.

EXPLORATION

This passage involves the death of a man Jesus cared for deeply, and Jesus' ministry to the sisters who remained. It is a story filled with both truth and grace.

The Death of Lazarus

So when Jesus came, He found that he had already been in the tomb four days. Now Bethany was near Jerusalem, about two miles away. And many of the Jews had joined the women around Martha and Mary, to comfort them concerning their brother.

Now Martha, as soon as she heard that Jesus was coming, went and met Him, but Mary was sitting in the house. Now Martha said to Jesus, "Lord, if You had been here, my brother would not have died. But even now I know that whatever You ask of God, God will give You."

Jesus said to her, "Your brother will rise again."

Martha said to Him, "I know that he will rise again in the resurrection at the last day."

Jesus said to her, "I am the resurrection and the life. He who believes in Me, though he may die, he shall live. And whoever lives and believes in Me shall never die. Do you believe this?"

She said to Him, "Yes, Lord, I believe that You are the Christ, the Son of God, who is to come into the world."

And when she had said these things, she went her way and secretly called Mary her sister, saying, "The Teacher has come and is calling for you." As soon as she heard that, she arose quickly and came to Him. Now Jesus had not yet come into the town, but was in the place where Martha met Him. Then the Jews who were with her in the house, and comforting her, when they saw that Mary rose up quickly and went out, followed her, saying, "She is going to the tomb to weep there."

Then, when Mary came where Jesus was, and saw Him, she fell down at His feet, saying to Him, "Lord, if You had been here, my brother would not have died."

Therefore, when Jesus saw her weeping, and the Jews who came with her weeping, He groaned in the spirit and was troubled. (John 11:17–33)

It is a comfort to see Jesus moved by the grief of Mary and Martha. He does not chastise us for wanting "our wills," but is deeply moved in spirit and troubled. Yes, it is His will that ultimately is done, but that doesn't mean His heart is immune to our tears. He is well acquainted with grief. Does this comfort you? Surprise you? Cause some other reaction?

VIDEO

If you'd like to take a few notes as you watch the session 4 video segment, use the space below.

REFLECTION

During this section it is time to open up and discover how God might use this session to transform your life.

Same as Me

➤ We all have them: remembrances of those times when we pleaded in faith, believing, and the spouse still died, the check never arrived, the friend refused to be reconciled. Briefly share one of your Lazarus stories.

➤ If your story is recent, it may still be too fresh to see the workings of God. But if some time has passed, you may have begun to see traces of God's hand and what Denver called the "something new" beginning. Share what you can of that with the group.

Different than Me

➤ When your Lazarus situation occurred, what were your feelings toward God? Did you feel abandoned? Angry? Disappointed? Confused?

➤ How long did you stay in the ditch of "if"? Are you still there?

THE REAL WORLD

Try this: *For the next week, only pray the Lord's Prayer.* You can pray it as many times a day as you like, but use only those words and phrases the Lord taught us. Keep a pen and paper handy, and record how it felt to limit your words to those lines. Also make a note of any experiences that directly tracked with the lines of the prayer.

Conclude this week's session by praying the Lord's Prayer together. And there's no law against circling up and joining hands either.

Our Father in heaven,
Hallowed be Your name.
Your kingdom come.
Your will be done
On earth as it is in heaven.
Give us this day our daily bread.
And forgive us our debts,
As we forgive our debtors.
And do not lead us into temptation,
But deliver us from the evil one.
For Yours is the kingdom and the power and the glory
forever. Amen.

blessing versus service

INTRODUCTION

When it comes to the poor or homeless, most people attempt to minister to them by blessing them. This is essentially a onetime act, like serving food on Thanksgiving or possibly writing a check—something that happens and then it's over. Serving "God's people," as Debbie called them, is something radically different. It is crawling down into whatever pit they're in and sticking around to help them in whatever way you can until they're strong enough to crawl out on your shoulders. As Ron learned in his experience with Denver, you'll never change someone's life unless you're willing to love that person. And that means hanging in there for the long haul—no *catch and release* allowed.

"I shall pass through this world but once. Any good therefore that I can do or any kindness that I can show to any human being, let me do it now."
—**Stephen Grellet**

GETTING STARTED

In the following excerpts, "service" is the common thread. What Ron discovers is that serving the least of these is like a multi-faceted gem; there are many ways of looking at it. Sometimes serving even means trusting another with your most prized possessions. Denver learned that same lesson, that serving Mr. Ron meant trusting that at the end of the day, we're not quite as different as we usually think. We're all looking for a friend.

OPENING CHAPTERS

Regan had finally found a job she was sure she'd love, as a cook for Young Life, a Christian youth camp. It was half the pay and twice the hours she worked at the gallery, but it was ministry work and it was in Colorado, set against the majestic Rockies, where a lot of twenty-five-year-olds feel called to suffer for the Lord.

Deborah felt strongly that Regan shouldn't hover around home, waiting to see how the cancer would progress. We encouraged her to take the job. So she packed her bags and headed west to the Crooked Creek Ranch in Winter Park, Colorado. But at twenty-five, Regan had more than luggage, having had apartments in both New York and Dallas.

Jokingly, I said to Denver one day, "Now that you've got a driver's license, would you like to drive Regan's things to Colorado?"

When I mentioned the route wound through the capital city of Denver, his smile stretched wider than an eight-lane interstate. "I always wanted to see the city I was named after," he said.

Now I'd opened my trap and couldn't take it back. So over the next three days, we hammered out a plan. I pulled out a road atlas and traced the route to Winter Park with colored marking pens. But Denver couldn't read the words in the atlas, so on plain paper, I drew a rough map with pictures of highway signs, and showed him what the one going to Colorado looked like. Denver was thoroughly convinced he could follow a map—and he convinced me as well.

So on a brilliant October day, we loaded my nearly new F-350 crew-cab pickup with everything Regan owned—TVs, stereos, clothes, furniture. We set a meeting time for him and Regan, 6:00 p.m. the following day at the Safeway grocery store in Winter Park. And after a final one-hour cram session, I sent him on his way, armed with $700 cash, a simple little hand-drawn map with checkpoints, phone numbers to call if he got in trouble, and a $30,000 truck with a free and clear title.

As he eased down the driveway, I ran alongside the truck, repeating, "Two-eighty-seven! Two-eighty-seven!" If he made the turn onto Highway 287, he'd be on his way to Colorado. If he missed it, he'd wind up in the hinterlands of Oklahoma where, I had tried to convince him, humans spoke an entirely different language.

I tried to convince myself I knew what I was doing, but the plain facts were that Denver was heading out on a two-thousand-mile round-trip, navigating interstates, back roads, and mountain passes—the highest in Colorado—using a driver's license that had arrived in the mail only the week before. What was he thinking? Better yet, what was *I* thinking?

As he pulled away with the money, my truck, and everything Regan owned, Denver wiped his forehead with the towel that he usually carried, grinning a little semi-grin that I couldn't quite decode.

The angel on my right shoulder whispered that it meant, "Thank you, Mr. Ron, for trustin me."

The devil on my left cackled, "No, it means 'Adiós, sucker!'"

* * *

I do some travelin, too. In January 2005, me and Mr. Ron went to the presidential inauguration. Mr. Ron was invited and he asked me to go with him. That was the first time I ever went on a airplane. We landed in a snowstorm, but I didn't know I was s'posed to be scared.

So there we was, on the White House lawn, sittin on the front row, and I'm lookin around at all the astronauts and war heroes and wonderin, how in the world did a fella like me wind up in a place like this? It was somethin I never even dreamed of. I wadn't that far from the president, but I wanted to check him out a li'l better so I got up outta my seat and walked up closer to where he was sittin, gettin ready to make his speech. But this Secret Service man, a black fella like me, held up his hand.

"Sir, where are you going?"

"I'm gon' walk right up here and see the president," I said.

He looked at me kinda firm. "No. You're close enough."

Later that night, me and Mr. Ron went to the inaugural ball. The president and his wife was dancin right there in front of me. I had on a tuxedo and a bow tie. I felt purty good about that.

The next day, I got to stand on the steps at the Lincoln Memorial. I remember way back when I was li'l bitty fella, Big Mama told me 'bout how President Lincoln freed black people from slavery. That's why they shot him.

I felt mighty blessed to be able to go and see the president. Me and Mr. Ron done some other travelin, too. I been to Santa Fe and San Diego. Back home in Dallas, we still go to restaurants and cafés, the ranch and rodeos, and to church on Sundays. All in all, we's purty tight. Lotta times, we'll sit out on the back porch at the Murchison place, or out on the patio at Rocky Top, lookin at the moon shinin on the river and talkin about life. Mr. Ron's still got a lot to learn.

I'm just messin with you. Even though I'm almost seventy years old, I got a lot to learn, too. I used to spend a lotta time worryin that I was different from other people, even from other homeless folks. Then, after I met Miss Debbie and Mr. Ron, I worried that I was so different from them that we wadn't ever gon' have no kind a' future. But I found out everybody's different—the same kind of different as me. We're all just regular folks walkin down the road God done set in front of us.

The truth about it is, whether we is rich or poor or somethin in between, this earth ain't no final restin place. So in a way, we is all homeless—just workin our way toward home.

ONE-LINER

Read the following statement and move right into the
Exploration section; then discuss as a group.

*"Coincidences are God's way of
remaining anonymous."*
—Ron Hall

EXPLORATION

Chances are good this passage is somewhat familiar. Still,
listen closely as a group member reads so you can join in
the exercise to follow in the reflection session. This could
conceivably be the scripture passage that best captures
the spirit of this entire study.

The Least of These

"Then the King will say to those on His right hand, 'Come, you blessed of My Father, inherit the kingdom prepared for you from the foundation of the world: for I was hungry and you gave Me food; I was thirsty and you gave Me drink; I was a stranger and you took Me in; I was naked and you clothed Me; I was sick and you visited Me; I was in prison and you came to Me.'

"Then the righteous will answer Him, saying, 'Lord, when did we see You hungry and feed You, or thirsty and give You drink? When did we see You a stranger and take You in, or naked and clothe You? Or when did we see You sick, or in prison, and come to You?' And the King will answer and say to them, 'Assuredly, I say to you, inasmuch as you did it to one of the least of these My brethren, you did it to Me.'" (Matthew 25:34–40)

As a group, talk through what comes to mind when you hear the phrase "the least of these."

VIDEO

If you'd like to take a few notes as you watch the session 5 video segment, use the space below.

REFLECTION

For something a little different in this last session, use the space below to rewrite these lines in your own words. Put them in the context of your daily life, being as specific as you can. (For example: *I lost my job, and you paid my rent for three months.*) These can be experiences when you ministered to the "least of these," or times when you were one of them. When you've finished, share a few lines with the group.

"For I was hungry and you gave Me food; I was thirsty and you gave Me drink; I was a stranger and you took Me in; I was naked and you clothed Me; I was sick and you visited Me; I was in prison and you came to Me."

THE REAL WORLD

Denver was amazed at how it seemed all white folk had "Bible studies." After a few times attending and speaking at these gatherings, he asked Ron, "Do they ever have any Bible doin's?" Look back over "The Real World" sections of this guide and evaluate how your "doin's" have been. Have they gone as you expected? Has each one held its own surprise? What have you learned? Don't give yourself a grade or anything, but share with the group how you've felt about this stepping out in the real world, the world God loves so very much.

Now turn the page to find **A Final Word**. These **Opening Chapter** and **The Real World** pieces are grace notes on your study together. As a group member reads, consider the reading to be a form of prayer. At the conclusion of the reading, a group "Amen!" is the equivalent of "Yes! We agree!"

"For God so loved the world that He gave His only begotten Son, that whoever believes in Him should not perish but have everlasting life."

—John 3:16

a final word

As the service began and the tiny congregation filled the air with old spirituals, Denver and I huddled on the back row. Pastor Tom had wanted me to introduce Denver from the pulpit but spend a few minutes telling his life story first. As I suspected, Denver wasn't having any of that. During the singing, he and I huddled on the back row to negotiate.

"It ain't nobody's business how I got here!" he whispered. "'Sides, I don't want to tell em 'bout me. I want to tell em 'bout the Lord."

"So what do you want me to say?"

He paused and stared down at the Bible laying on the bench next to me. "Just tell em I'm a nobody that's tryin to tell everbody 'bout Somebody that can save *anybody*. That's all you need to tell em."

And so, when the singing stopped, I walked down front and said just that. Then Denver took the pulpit. At first, his voice quavered a bit, but it was loud.

And the longer he preached, the louder and stronger it became. And like a magnet, his voice pulled people in off the street. By the time he wiped the sweat off his face and sat down, the pews were nearly full.

Like a cannonball, Pastor Tom shot out of his seat into the pulpit, raising his arms toward the people. "I believe God wants Denver to come back and preach a revival!" he said. The congregation, most of whom had been drawn into the sanctuary by Denver's voice, exploded into applause.

My mind flashed to Deborah's dream, her seeing Denver's face, and recalling the words of Solomon: *There was found in the city a certain poor man who was wise and by his wisdom he saved the city.*

Again, something new had begun. Something I was certain had my wife dancing for joy on streets of gold.

THE REAL WORLD

You may still be unsure of exactly what God is asking you to do in regard to the homelessness that exists in our land. That's all right. Your commitment to this study and this group of people is a huge step in the right direction; you're ahead of the pack. As you go from this point on, don't forget that at the end of the day, relationships are the only thing that will heal and cure homelessness; in other words, being a friend that won't catch and release, being a friend forever. The truth about it is, as Denver said, "Whether we is rich or poor or somethin in between, this earth ain't no final restin place. So in a way, we is all homeless—just workin our way toward home."